D0506872

AlphaBasiCs

Everyday STRUCTURES

from
A
to
Z

Bobbie Kalman

 Crabtree Publishing Company

Created by Bobbie Kalman

For my friend Maarika Maury

Author and Editor-in-Chief
Bobbie Kalman

Managing editor
Lynda Hale

Research and editing team
April Fast
Kate Calder
Jane Lewis
Heather Levigne
Hannelore Sotzek

Computer design
Lynda Hale
John Crossingham (borders & letters)

Production coordinator
Hannelore Sotzek

Separations and film
Dot 'n Line Image Inc.

Printer
Worzalla Publishing Company

Special thanks to
The students of Michael J. Brennan and Pine Grove Elementary School, Peter Crabtree, Joan King

Photographs
Jim Bryant: page 13 (top left); Marc Crabtree: pages 3, 5 (bottom), 15 (bottom left), 20 (right), 21 (top left), 25 (bottom left), 28 (middle), 29 (top right); Lori Hale: page 13 (bottom left); Susan Hughes: pages 13 (top), 28 (top); Wolfgang Kaehler: page 23 (top right); Bobbie Kalman: pages 19 (bottom left), 21 (bottom left); other images by Digital Stock and Eyewire, Inc.

Illustrations
Barbara Bedell: pages 17, 19 (cells), 22, 24, 30; Halina Below: page 31 (top); Antoinette "Cookie" Bortolon: pages 19 (boy), 27; © Crabtree Publishing Company: pages 4, 6, 7 (bottom), 8, 14, 16, 18, 26, 29, 31 (top); Jeannette McNaughton-Julich: page 28 (wheels); Trevor Morgan: pages 7 (top), 12; Bonna Rouse: page 31 (zipper); Moira Tasker: page 28 (right)

Crabtree Publishing Company

PMB 16A	360 York Road	73 Lime Walk
350 Fifth Avenue,	RR 4	Headington,
Suite 3308	Niagara-on-the-Lake	Oxford
New York, NY	Ontario, Canada	OX3 7AD
10118	L0S 1J0	United Kingdom

Cataloging in Publication Data

Kalman, Bobbie
  Everyday structures from A to Z

(AlphaBasiCs)
Includes index.

ISBN 0-86505-387-1 (library bound) ISBN 0-86505-417-7 (pbk.)
This book is an alphabetical introduction to the properties of natural and human-made structures, discussing form versus function and how structures are built.

1. Structural engineering—Juvenile literature. [1. Structural engineering. 2. Building. 3. Alphabet.] I. Title. II. Series. Kalman, Bobbie. AlphaBasiCs.

TA634.K36 2000   j624   LC 99-42505
                                                          CIP

Contents

is for **about structures**. A structure is made up of different parts. The parts are put together in a way that suits the purpose of each structure. Structures come in all sizes and shapes. Some are made up of many shapes. An **artificial** structure, such as a building, is made by people. A **natural** structure is not made by people. It is found in nature. List the natural and artificial structures on this page.

(top left) Your body is a natural structure. Did you know that, like this popsicle, your body is made mostly of water? (top right) A tree is a natural structure, but a tree house is not. What kind of structure is it? (left) Are flowers and butterfly wings natural or artificial structures? What colors do you see in these petals and wings?

is for **buildings**. Buildings are artificial structures that give **shelter** from wind, rain, and snow. Buildings come in different shapes and have many uses. They can be houses, apartments, or office towers. Schools, hospitals, and shopping malls are other kinds of buildings. In which kind of building do you live? Is it a big or small building? In which kind of building do some animals live?

(top left) Did you guess that some animals live in a barn? What shape is the structure beside the barn? What do you think is inside?
*(top right) The **foundation** is the lowest part of a building. It **supports**, or holds up, the rest of the house. An architect has drawn the plans for this house.*
(left) Name five kinds of buildings in a city.

5

is for **construction**. Construction means putting parts together to make a structure. Construction workers need tools and machines to construct buildings, roads, and bridges. They use **materials** such as brick, wood, glass, and cement to construct houses and other buildings. Look at the materials these workers are using. Which material came from trees? Which material can you see through?

These workers are laying bricks on the outside of this house by joining them together with a cement mixture. Other workers are covering the roof with shingles to protect it from rain and snow.

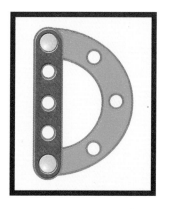

is for **domes**. Domes are buildings or parts of buildings that look like upside-down bowls. Snow buildings called **igloos** are dome-shaped. Many sports arenas are also dome-shaped. Domes are often found on houses, government buildings, and churches.

Find six domes in this picture. Which domed structure do you think is a government building? Which is a theater? How many dome-shaped trees can you count? Discover the domes in your neighborhood!

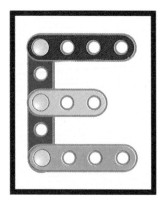

is for **everyday structures**. Every day, everywhere you look, you see structures. Structures are all around you. Fences, trees, furniture, and teeter-totters are all structures. There are structures inside and outside your home and school. Their shape and size can tell you how each one is used. Point to ten structures in this picture and describe how each one is used. How many have domes?

(above) Chairs are built so people can sit on them. How are tables different from chairs?
(right) Name the parts of a bicycle that make it move.

(above) Boats are structures built to float on water. Which natural structures are able to float?

(above) How does this structure help keep this boy safe? What might happen without it?
(left) Some structures are called **instruments**. What is this musical instrument called? Name five other musical instruments.

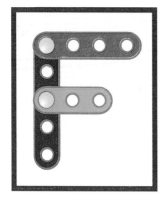

is for **famous structures**. Many structures are ordinary, but others are one-of-a-kind. These unique structures are famous because they have special designs. Castles, pyramids, statues, and towers are some kinds of famous structures. The Great Wall of China is the only human-made structure on Earth that can be seen from the Moon! Which famous structures do you know?

(above) This famous fairy-tale castle is in Germany. How many **towers** does it have?
(below) To build the Great Wall, many walls were **connected**, or joined, to make one large structure. Is the wall long or short? Is it old or new?

(top) Pyramids have an unusual shape. What is it? How many sides do they have?
(bottom) The Taj Mahal in India is **symmetrical**, or the same on both sides. Point to its center.

is for **geometric shapes**. Every structure has a shape. Some structures are made up of many shapes. Shapes that have circles and straight lines are called geometric shapes. Triangles, circles, ovals, rectangles, squares, cylinders, diamonds, hexagons, and octagons are some geometric shapes. Using different shapes can make structures strong. Shapes also make structures look interesting.

*Look at the geometric shapes at the side and bottom of this page. How many do you know? When shapes are repeated, they form a **pattern**. Which geometric shapes and patterns can you find in these photographs? Which colors are used to make the patterns? Create your own patterns using different colors and shapes.*

square

octagon

circle

hexagon

cylinder

pentagon

oval

diamond

rectangle

triangle

is for **homes**. Homes are structures in which people or animals live. Nests are homes made by birds. Foxes and bears make their homes in **dens**. A **beehive** is home to hundreds of bees, and a **mound** is home to thousands of termites. Beavers live in **lodges** that they build on water, and prairie dogs and desert tortoises dig **tunnel** homes.

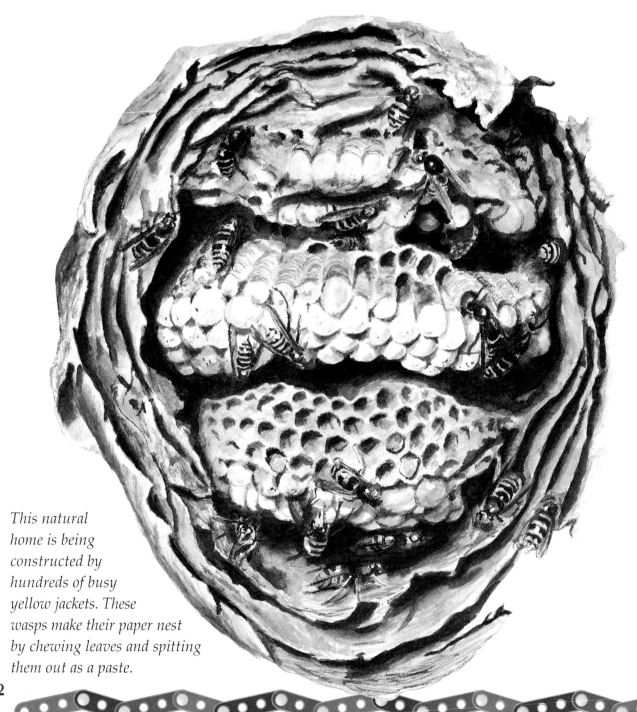

This natural home is being constructed by hundreds of busy yellow jackets. These wasps make their paper nest by chewing leaves and spitting them out as a paste.

People also live in many kinds of homes. Homes can be big, small, plain, or fancy. People build homes to stay warm and safe. They design their homes to suit the places in which they live. They use materials such as mud, stone, wood, and brick. Some homes have a foundation, walls, ceilings, doors, windows, and stairs. Which of these homes have no windows or stairs?

(top left) Why do you think people used mud and grass to build their rainforest home? (top right) Some people live and work on boats. (bottom right) In cities, many people live in apartments. (left) Some homes are built on **stilts**, *or poles, for protection from animals or to keep the building dry during the rainy season. How do stilts help do both these things?*

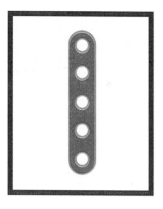

is for **interior**, or inside. The inside of a structure is different from the outside. The outside of a structure has to be strong enough to withstand hot and cold weather. Inside, people like to have comfortable, attractive rooms. They **decorate** with furniture and pictures. Some paint the interior of their homes. The girl on the left is choosing her curtains and bedspread from samples of fabric.

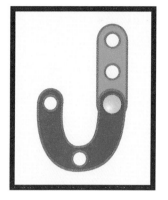

is for **join**. Parts of structures join, or come together, at **joints**. Some joints allow the parts to bend and move. Your elbows, knees and ankles are joints that allow your arms and legs to move. **Bridging** means joining two structures. Bridges are structures that connect, or join, two pieces of land so that people can travel from one to the other. They are built over water, highways, or between two buildings.

(above) Bridges allow people to travel over water.
(below) These arches join together to support the ceiling of this temple.

(above) This woman is able to jump and skate because she can bend her knees, ankles, elbows, and wrists. Joints also allow us to move our hips, neck, mouth, fingers, and toes.

K is for **kinds of structures**. There are three kinds of structures—**shell** structures, **frame** structures, and **solid** structures. Each kind of structure has a different purpose. A shell structure is **hollow** inside. A solid structure is made of the same material inside and outside. A frame structure is supported by a frame such as a skeleton. A skeleton supports your **muscles** and **organs**.

(above) Some shell structures hold things. The shell provides a cover to protect its contents. A tent is a shell structure, but it also has a metal frame.

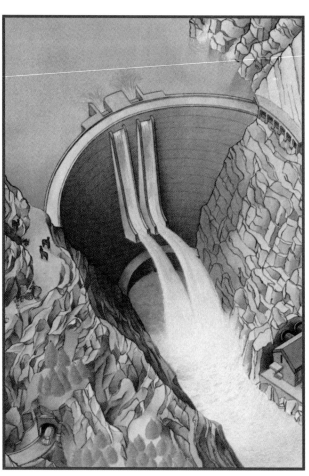

*(above) A wall is an artificial structure made of bricks or stones. A **dam** is a wall that stops the flow of water on one side. Rocks are natural solid structures.*

(left) Frame structures are made of parts that fit together or hold other parts in place. A bridge is a frame structure. It supports a road. A house is also a frame structure. Its frame supports its walls and roof.

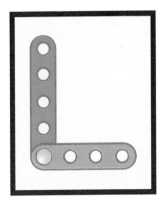

is for **landforms.** Landforms cover the Earth's surface. Mountains, valleys, and plains are all landforms. They are created by weather and the movement of **plates**, or huge rocky pieces, under the Earth's surface. When a river runs down a mountain for thousands of years, it **erodes**, or wears down the rock and creates deep canyons. Wind also erodes rock and wears down mountains.

(top left) Some mountains are formed when one plate moves under another and forces up the rock above it.
(top right) Rushing water erodes rock.
(bottom left) The Grand Canyon was formed over the past ten million years by rushing water.
(bottom right) This interesting landform was carved by blowing wind and soil.

is for **measuring**. People use words to describe the parts of a structure they are measuring. If they are measuring a structure with sides, people might talk about its **length**, **width**, and **height**. Measuring a circle, they would use words such as **circumference**, **radius**, and **diameter**. To measure the amount of a liquid inside a structure, people might use the word **volume** or **depth**.

This girl's father is measuring how much she has grown in the last year. Is he measuring her width, height, or circumference? You are right! He is measuring her height.

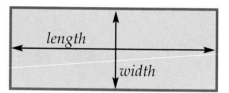

The length is the measurement across the longer side of an object. The width is the shorter side.

Is this boy showing the length or depth of this pool?

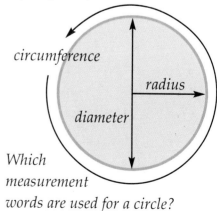

Which measurement words are used for a circle?

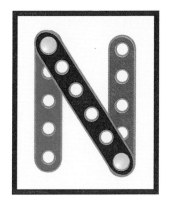

is for **natural structures**. Natural structures are not built by people. They are a part of nature. Many natural structures are living things. They need water, food, and air to survive. Your body is a natural structure. It is made up of tiny **cells**. Cells grow, change, and die. All living structures are made of cells. Some are made up of just one, and others have millions of cells.

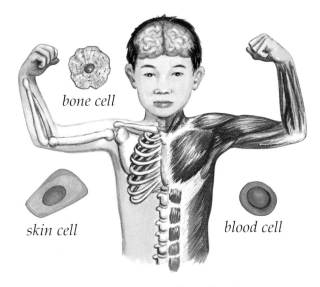

bone cell

skin cell

blood cell

Natural structures can be **stiff** or **flexible**. Flexible means something bends easily. Is your body flexible?

(above) Natural structures have many shapes and **textures**. Texture is how something feels when you touch it. What is the shape of a sea star? Is its texture rough or smooth? Is your skin rough or smooth?

(below) Some structures make a sound. What sound can you hear in a seashell?

People copy natural structures to make artificial structures such as machines. These tall cranes look a lot like giraffes. Both giraffes and cranes can reach high in the air.

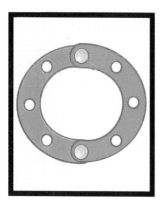

is for **ornaments**. Ornaments are decorations. Some ornaments are structures. Statues of famous people are **ornamental** structures. Other ornaments decorate buildings or parts of structures. They include carvings, pictures, columns, or towers and are often painted with bright colors. They make structures look attractive. People use their imagination to create ornaments.

*(above) This building has decorative, triangular structures called **gables**. How many gables can you count?*

(left) Some ornamental structures, such as this giant statue, are sacred. (above) This picture shows the door of a community center, which has been decorated to look like a face.

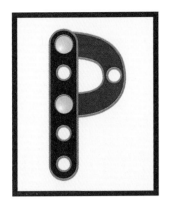

is for **playground structures**. Playground structures are built for climbing, swinging, hanging, running, splashing, and jumping. They are a lot of fun! What kinds of structures are there in your school playground or park? Look at all the geometric shapes that make up these structures and name five. Some structures are solid, and some contain **liquids**. Which playground structure contains a liquid?

(above) This playground has several structures to explore. There are many shapes and textures to discover.
(right) Some slides are smooth. This one has a bumpy texture.

(above) This fancy structure has a bridge. How would you design a playground structure?
(left) Some playground structures are frames for climbing.

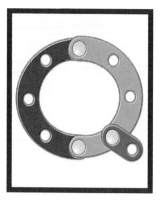

is for **questions**. To learn about the structures around us, we ask questions about them. We examine how structures are the same and how they are different from one another. When you look at a structure, ask these questions:

How tall is it? How wide is it? What shape is it? What is it made of? What does it do? Is it old or new? Is it an artificial structure or a natural structure? How does it help people or animals? Is it a solid structure, frame structure, or shell structure? Does it have joints that allow it to move? Is it symmetrical?

is for **religious structures**. Churches, temples, and mosques are buildings in which religious services are held. Religious structures are often large and have steeples, domes, pillars, and towers.

People often decorate the structures in which they worship to show love and respect.
(left) The religious structure in this picture is called a **mosque**. *It is a house of worship for those who follow a religion called Islam.*
(top right) The interior of this temple is decorated with golden statues and other ornaments.
(bottom right) This huge church is called a **cathedral***.*

is for **space structures**. Planets, moons, meteors, and stars are natural structures in space. Space probes, satellites, space shuttles, and space stations are artificial structures that are sent into space by people. Many of them **orbit**, or travel around, Earth or another planet. They send information back to scientists on Earth. Space structures help scientists study Earth and other planets and moons.

The space shuttle has a giant mechanical arm with several joints that allow it to bend and grasp objects.

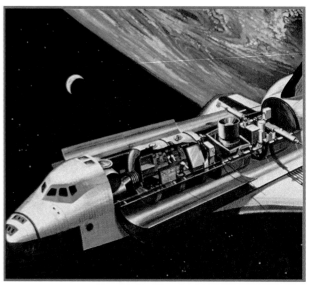

A space shuttle has a lab in which scientists conduct experiments.

*Satellites receive radio signals with an **antenna**, or a disk on a rod. The structures on either side are solar panels that gather the sun's light to use as energy.*

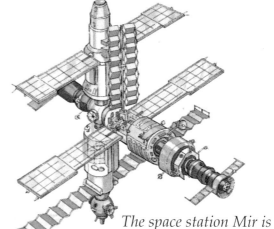

The space station Mir is a structure designed for conducting experiments in space for a long period of time. It has a lab, living quarters, a satellite antenna, and large solar panels for heating.

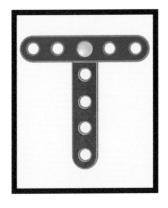

is for **towers**. Towers are structures that are taller than they are wide. They can be shaped like a rectangle, a tube, or a narrow triangle. Towers can stand alone or be part of a building. They give people a view of the land from high above or send messages to people far away. Lighthouse towers have a bright light that helps people on boats locate the shore. Clock towers show the time.

Match each of these towers with a phrase below.

1. *On a lean in Italy.*
2. *A giant piece of art in Paris.*
3. *The world's tallest radio signal.*
4. *What time is it in London?*
5. *A ship captain's guiding light.*
6. *Welcome to North America!*

Answers: 1E, 2C, 3F, 4B, 5A, 6D

is for **underground structures**. A cave is a natural underground structure. It is a hollow space below the ground. Most caves are formed over thousands of years as rainwater trickles down through cracks in the Earth. The water **dissolves**, or mixes with, large areas of underground **limestone**. Tunnels and passages are formed, water collects into pools, and rivers flow underground.

*(above) Caves contain structures called **stalactites** that look like icicles. They form when water mixed with limestone drips from the ceiling of a cave. Water also forms cone-shaped **stalagmites** that build up from the floor of the cave.*

*(left) A **subway** is a human-made underground tunnel through which trains travel. Most subways are in large cities. Many people use subways to get from place to place quickly.*

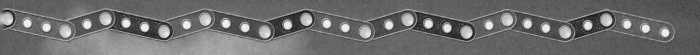

is for **volcano**. A volcano is a **vent**, or crack, in the Earth's surface. The Earth's surface is called the **crust**. It is a thin layer of rock. Underneath the crust is a thick layer of rock called the **mantle**. **Magma** is found in the mantle. Magma is **molten**, or melted, rock. Sometimes it pushes its way through the crust through volcanoes. The **core**, or center, of the Earth lies beneath the mantle.

ash

vent
(volcano)

lava

magma

When magma pushes through Earth's surface, it is called *lava*. The lava cools and hardens into a new layer of rock around the volcano. Over time, more layers are added, and the volcano slowly grows into a mountain.

is for **wheel**. The wheel is an important structure that was invented 5000 years ago. Before wheels were made, people put heavy objects on logs to roll them from place to place. The first wheels were circles cut from blocks of wood. The **rim**, or edge, was covered with a strip of leather or metal. Those strips were the first tires! Today we use wheels in many ways. Think of ten ways you use wheels every day.

People discovered that it was easier to move heavy objects by rolling them over logs. The idea of rolling led to the invention of the wheel.

The first wheels were round disks of solid wood.

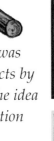

Wooden wheels with spokes were bigger but lighter.

Now wheels have a tire made of rubber. The inside of the wheel has a tube filled with air.

We need wheels for many types of transportation. Which of these pictures show fun ways of moving around on wheels?

is for **eXciting structures**. Roller coasters and ferris wheels are structures that are exciting to watch and ride. They are exciting because they take people high up in the air, drop them down quickly, or spin them around fast. Roller coasters zoom down steep hills and speed around corners to give people a thrilling ride. Carousels move children around and around on brightly colored animal statues.

(top left) If you were to create some structures for the future, how would they look? Would you create giant robots and miniature spaceships?

(above) These people are about to have the ride of their life. Hold on tight! Wheeeeeeee...

(left) Some fun structures go at a slower pace than others. The carousel takes people for a gentle ride with delightful music and twinkling lights. Is the ferris wheel one of your favorite rides? Do you like heights?

29

is for **your structures**. What kinds of structures do you like to build? Why? What materials do you use? What is the smallest structure you have built? What is the biggest? Have you built something that is taller than yourself? Have you ever built a structure that floats or flies?

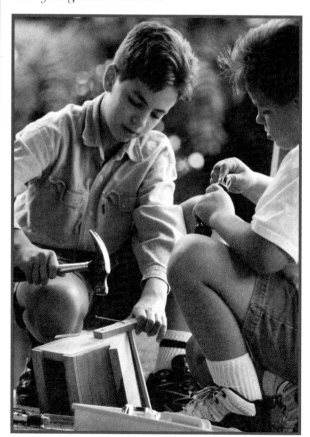

(above) Molly is building a structure out of wood. She is balancing both sides so it will not fall over. Will her structure stay upright? (below) Nick and Josh are building a structure that has an important function. They are using a hammer and nails to attach pieces of wood together. They have instructions that show them the steps of building this structure. Can you guess what it is?

Robin is experimenting to see how high she can stack her blocks. How soon will her tower of blocks tumble down?

mast → sail
crossbar
cargo hold
base

To build this raft, you will need flat sticks, glue, and paper. Lay ten sticks side by side to make the base of the raft. Glue two sticks on top of each other at either end of the base to create **crossbars**. Place a heavy book on top until the glue dries. Glue a third crossbar beside the first. Make a mast by gluing together two sticks in the shape of a T. When the mast is dry, push it between the two crossbars. Cut a piece of paper for a sail, and glue the bottom edge to the crossbar and the top edge to the top of the mast. Glue two sticks across the open ends of the raft for railings.

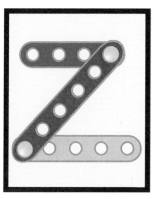

is for **zigzag**. A zigzag is a pattern made by lines that change direction, as in the letter Z. It can be seen in many structures. Find zigzags in your clothes, home, and school yard.

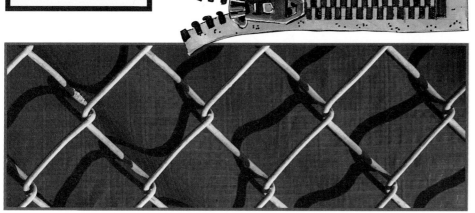

Words to know

cathedral A large church

cell The basic part of every living thing; most plants and animals are made of millions of connected cells

circumference The distance around the outside of a circle

decorate To add ornaments in order to make something look attractive

design A pattern used to construct something

diameter The distance across a circle, passing through the center

limestone A type of rock found in underground caves that is often used for making cement

liquid A runny substance, such as water, which flows easily

material A substance that is used to make things

muscles The tissues and fibers in a body that enable the body to move

orbit To travel around a planet or star

organ A part of the body that does a special job. For example, the heart pumps blood throughout the body.

plate One of the many pieces of Earth's crust

radius The distance from the center to the outside of a circle

shelter A covering that protects people or animals from wind, rain, or snow

volume The amount of space taken up by an object or liquid

Index

1 2 3 4 5 6 7 8 9 0 Printed in the U.S.A. 8 7 6 5 4 3 2 1 0 9